Capenter

W9-BIO-170

JOSH McDOWELL

& PAUL LEWIS

Givers, Takers & other kinds of Lovers

TYNDALE HOUSE PUBLISHERS, INC. WHEATON, ILLINOIS

All Scripture
quotations
are from the
*New American
Standard Bible,*
unless otherwise
indicated.

Library of Congress
Catalog Card Number
79-91985
ISBN 0-8423-1033-9,
cloth
ISBN 0-8423-1032-0,
special edition
Copyright © 1980
by Josh McDowell
and Paul Lewis
All rights reserved.

First printing,
April 1980
Printed in the
United States
of America.

To
Jim and Vivian Simpson
who have enjoyed and shared
the secret of loving for
thirty-eight years

CONTENTS

1
WHAT KIND OF LOVE DO YOU WANT?

♥

Rich . . .vigorous . . .enduring and satisfying LOVE! You want it. I want it. Without it, our lives are at best incomplete—at worst, desperate. The yearning to give and receive robust, unending love throbs in the heart of every one of us.

An ancient Jewish apostle described this love we seek. He wrote:

Love is so patient and so kind;
Love never boils with jealousy;
It never boasts, is never puffed with pride;
It does not act with rudeness, or insist upon its rights;
It never gets provoked, it never harbors evil thoughts;
Is never glad when wrong is done,
But always glad when truth prevails;
It bears up under anything,

It exercises faith in everything,
It keeps up hope in everything,
It gives us power to endure in anything.
Love never fails. (1 Cor. 13:4-8, Williams)

And after two thousand more years of loving,
no one has improved on that. It's still the
love for which we search.

This pursuit of love has caused more heartache and pain than all the diseases and
wars of history. There's no limit to what you
and I will do to express true love...and
to feel it for ourselves. We can't live *without* it.

Unfortunately, we don't seem able to
live *with* it either. At least, not with the sort
of love we've found thus far. The prevailing
notion is that love comes gift-wrapped in sex.
And sex does seem to be the perfect complement—the door to genuine, satisfying
love. What better bedfellows? Both sex and
love stir the marvelous passions that lie
deep within us.

Is sex the secret?

Lovers come in an incredibly wide assort-
ment. And why not? To some, it's an intricate
and challenging game of strategy, and
they're busy learning all the rules. Some
become real polished players. Others are
still looking for the square marked "start."
And you? You're in there somewhere.

Several years ago, I met Paul Lewis when
we happened to be dating twin sisters. Our

friendship has been a deep and enduring one. And at the time we met, something else happened, too. We both began to recognize and understand what real love is all about. Those two sisters and their folks modeled to us a love anyone would envy. That's why this book is dedicated to Mom and Dad Simpson.

In time Paul married one of those sisters, Leslie. And eleven years of marriage have deepened their understanding of how to keep and nourish true love. That's why I asked Paul to join me in writing this book.

Later Dottie, my best friend and sweetheart, became my wife. And for nine years, we've enjoyed an equally creative and beautiful love together.

This book is titled, *Givers, Takers, and Other Kinds of Lovers* for a very good reason. People try in many ways to discover this rich, vigorous, and constantly growing love. Often we are persuaded that the secret is to become liberated and free from the puritanical restraints of the past. Well, I'm pleased to announce that we've all been free for quite a while. Even the memory of those repressive days has evaporated.

But I receive letters from all over the country, from young people as well as married adults, indicating that dynamic love is still missing for them. The yearning still burns unfulfilled. Maybe it's that way for you, too.

And shouldn't we ask why? Why, amid

the unlimited freedom for sexual expression we've now enjoyed for so long, are we still as dissatisfied and unfulfilled as ever? Why is something so natural and beautiful as sex turning out such poor relationships?

What's wrong? Is sex the secret of loving?

2
WHATEVER HAPPENED TO SEXUAL FREEDOM?

♥

Two years ago, *Time* magazine printed a cartoon to illustrate a feature article on "The New Morality." The cartoon showed two college-age women obviously involved in heavy conversation as they walked through a park. One woman said to the other, "To tell the truth, I wish I'd been born before sex."

While it's an extreme comment, there are fleeting moments when every one of us feels like that. We are bombarded with an overload of information on sex. From dawn 'til dusk, the images and words—some subtle, some blatant—blast away at us. Whether you read *Time, Ebony, Ladies' Home Journal, Playboy, Reader's Digest, Cosmopolitan, Redbook, Family Health, His, Campus Life, Harper's Bazaar, Psychology Today,* or *Human Behavior,* you'll likely find an article on sex. In one, you can read about "The Pleasures of Sexual Freedom" alongside "The Problems of Sexual Freedom." In another, a female clinical psychologist discusses "The Sexual Loneliness of the American Male." And if that doesn't turn you on, the next issue will have a male clinical psychologist telling women about "Self-confidence and Sex Appeal." We can read "How Important Is Sex in Marriage?" or "Getting More Joy Out of Sex." Single, married, old, young—sex is for us!

And television and movies rub in the same message. Whether it's the "jiggly" shows, sexually based advertisements for cars or romantic after-shave ("It arouses more than just your face"), the message is clear. Sexual freedom.

Writers and readers, producers and viewers —all are concerned with sexual liberty, sexual fulfillment, sexual pleasure, sexual fears, and sexual joys. The familiar authorities, Masters and Johnson, have an organization geared totally to sex research. And other investigators with less scientific methods and more sensual conclusions, flood the market with books which describe the latest in "love" techniques and body positions.

But sexual discussions aren't confined to print or movie and television screens. Wherever people gather they talk sex—in homes, college dorms, motel units, and

Chevy vans. And despite all the comments and questions, the "answers" are often fuzzy and tentative.

Is sexual performance the only issue?

With all the research and emphasis on sex, statisticians have had a field day. The Census Bureau informs us that over one million unmarried couples now live together—a 600 percent increase in this last decade. Pollsters have learned that more people are having sexual intercourse outside of marriage than ever before, and that they're doing it at a younger age. What was a good-night kiss twenty years ago has today become an evening of full disclosure. All this talk, freedom, and experimentation has put the pressure on young people to perform.

For some, increased sexual awareness has been liberating. For others, it's become downright devastating.

Among the "liberated" is Catherine Breslin, author of *The Mistress Condition: New Options in Sex, Love and Other Female Pleasures.* "Sex," she says, "is certainly a large part of the new game—rollicking, satisfying, non-exploitative sex, a grownup but playful sort of business." This "game" is self-fulfillment and gratification. The "new woman," she says, looks at life and sex from a different perspective than her older counterpart. Marriage to the new lady "looks like a strange and difficult, even burdensome, arrangement." One man can't meet all her needs. Says Breslin, "A mistress-of-her-own-life may have eight or ten important men she enjoys: One for jogging in the park, one for the opera, another for skiing, still another for gourmet cooking, and two or three for good sex, each of them a different sensual experience. Plus two or three good, loving friends—men she can tell anything to, and cry all over when times get rough."

How happy is the sexually liberated woman?

But what about this perspective? Does it produce happiness and fulfillment? Does sex as a game and "playful business" generate a sense of personal worth? Does having many men dissolve the reality of loneliness or take the place of a permanent, enduring relationship?

According to the research, the answer is no. Says Theodore I. Rubin, M.D., "Women often engage in sexual activity for nonsexual reasons. A woman goes out with a man and then goes to bed with him not because she wants to but because she feels that sex is expected and that she won't hear from him again unless she does. Sexual activity engaged in for this reason can make a woman feel unhappy—angry and guilty and used. If people engage in sex freely when they're not ready to, before they have sufficient self-esteem to decide whether they want to do it with a particular person or simply because they're told it's okay, that can lead to an increase in self-hate."

Feelings of anger, guilt, and being used—consumed with self-hate—are these the side-effects of liberation? Rubin is not the only one who is putting out warning signals. Clinical psychologist Lonnie Garfield Barbach, author of *For Yourself: The Fulfillment of Female Sexuality,* admits that the pressure may be greatest on younger women. Many of Barbach's patients feel that everyone is supposed to be "free, open, sensual, multi-orgasmic and without sexual inhibition." When they can't fulfill these expectations, they are "incredibly hard on themselves." She says, "These women in their twenties are torn between the rather conservative messages their parents whisper to them and the philosophy of the sexual revolution."

Men in the sexual trap

But it's not only the women who suffer. Dr. Karen Shanor, a clinical psychologist who studied male sexuality for two years and published her findings in *The Shanor Study,* says that "like the American woman, the American man is currently re-examining his traditional image [which, she says, is to function as the conquering stud, etc.] and finding that it severely limits his potential as a human being." More than half of the men Shanor surveyed "admitted that far from having a ball, they were dissatisfied with their sex lives. Why? There were many reasons, but I can sum up by saying that all too often, American men are caught in a no-man's land between the myth that no longer holds true (if, indeed, it ever did) and the dream that has not yet come true—the dream of a loving intimacy never to be achieved in a one-night stand. Men are, in a sense, on a journey from a bad place to a better one, but they have not yet reached their goal, and they are becoming increasingly conscious of the loneliness of the road."

Pop psychologist Dr. Joyce Brothers commented on this sexual pilgrimage in the *Time* magazine look at "the New Morality." Brothers said, "We're not as swinging a people as we think we are. People found that instant sex was about as satisfying as a sneeze. It takes a lot of time and trouble to have sex with a lot of people, and they found it wasn't even worth the scheduling." Barbara Seaman, author of *Free and Female,* is even more descriptive. "The backlash is against casual sex because a lot of people were hurt. It was as if there was a train gradually carrying us away from Victorian morality, but then suddenly in the 60s and

70s the train became a runaway and a lot of passengers were injured. Now the brakes are starting to be repaired."

The look after the leap

One person who got derailed, but not seriously injured (her diagnosis), was Gretchen Kurz. A student at San Jose State University, Gretchen talked very candidly in the August 1977 issue of *Mademoiselle* magazine. Says Gretchen, who entered school ready for the "decadent life." "There I was, well equipped with my No. 2 pencil, student service card and an adequate supply of birth control pills. But somehow, I missed the boat on the pleasure cruise to carefree, guiltfree sex. Actually, I now believe it's all a myth perpetuated by a lot of disappointed students too afraid to tell the truth. But then again, how are you supposed to admit it's all a crock after you couldn't wait to get out and break all the rules?"

Gretchen never doubted that when she got to San Jose State she'd "share" sex. But she says, "To put it mildly, 'share' was a gross misnomer. My first encounter with Mr. Variety-Is-the-Spice-of-Life left me utterly confused by a number of things. Do I leave now or spend the night? What will I say in the morning? Is it kosher to borrow his bathrobe? Was I any good? He wasn't.

Does this mean we've started something somewhat permanent?" She discovered it didn't. "To say that I was overcome by guilt would be a lie, but the experience was far from euphoric. The most positive description I could use to label the exchange would be 'dull.' It was void of emotion, or perhaps any trace of emotion was deftly disguised as avant-garde nonchalance. I soon found this cool and detached approach characteristic of any future encounters.

"This lack of emotion not only baffled me, it infuriated me. I wanted to know why it existed and why it was so instrumental in the sexual liberation of my college friends. Obviously, it was the all too common basis for an active sex life. . . ."

Disturbed, Gretchen began to ask the many men in her life why this detached unemotionalism existed. What was their view of sex? The answers were similar. Sex is "fun and games" . . . "a natural reaction" . . . "consenting adults and a good time." "Words like love, share and happy never entered the conversation."

She decided to return to "my celibate, but happy, style of life" and some time after making this decision, she talked to a close, male friend who was airing his gripes about the free and easy college sex circuit. In describing what he felt was the thinking of a majority of college males, he said, "Most of the times I found myself in bed with someone, I usually wished it never had gotten that far. After I reached a point where I knew I would wind up spending the night with her, it was all downhill. I just went through the motions. There were times when all I wanted was to hurry up and get it over with. I finally stopped messing around when I realized sex is no good unless there is a true trust and love involved. Without it, it's just not worth the hassle."

Gretchen concluded her article with these words, "Now, with all this fuss about sexual freedom, it's a little hard to stand up and admit it's not what everyone imagines, especially to an anxious world that refuses to let the subject die. Consequently, here we sit, tight-lipped, and too embarrassed to say we couldn't find it. We can't admit it to the world and, worse yet, to ourselves. Perhaps we could all begin to set the record straight—by saying that without love and trust, 'it's just not worth the hassle.' "

Where do we go from here?

Interesting, isn't it? Amid all the talk and practice of sexual freedom, liberation, and fulfillment, right here in the middle of the sexual revolution, we find a lot of casualties and phrases like, "a train that's been derailed," "about as satisfying as a sneeze," "as unemotional as a No. 2 pencil." Could

this be sex—the glorious, orgasmic,
emotional experience worshiped by the
masses? Something must have gone wrong.
Could there be more to maximum sex
than a rollicking game, "a playful business,"
a succession of lovers and one-night stands
or marriages gone sour?

Maybe love and trust are important. But on
what basis? And where does sex fit in?
Maybe sex is not the secret of loving.

Fortunately, there is an answer. One as
complete and realistic as it is positive
and happy. It's time to consider the source.

3
WHO THOUGHT UP SEX?

♥

For some time now, the Federal Drug Administration has required that all consumer products carry a label listing the ingredients they contain. Wouldn't it be great if sex had such a label—if there were a manufacturer's manual which explained how sex works and how we can get the most out of it?

Well, good news! There is such a manual. But you won't find it among the scores of sex technique volumes bursting the shelves of your local bookstore. The most comprehensive information on sex and loving ever put in print originated 3500 years ago with a fellow named Moses. Writing by divine assignment from the "Manufacturer," he set down the authoritative word about the origins and functions of sex. His book is called Genesis.

In the first two chapters, he describes the

process of original creation. And at the apex of that process, he writes, "God created man in His own image, . . .male and female He created them." And, there it is: sexuality has been a fundamental part of man from the very beginning—designed for man by God the Creator. One can't be human without being male or female.

A little later in chapter two, we learn just how uniquely man and woman were made for each other. After labeling all the rest of his creative acts "good," God said it was "not good" for man to be alone. And that's amazing. If anyone ever had the perfect environment, it was the first man—the ultimate example of God's creativity, living in God's perfect climate, walking with God himself in the cool of the evening, endowed with sufficient creativity to think up names for all the animals God had created. Yet something was missing. This man was still alone. He had the original built-in "urge to merge." And no amount of perfection could diminish that.

The perfect complement

So Moses tells us that God put Adam to sleep and fashioned a woman from one of his ribs. And for Adam it wasn't a side issue, either. In verse 23, Adam wakes up, sees the woman, and says, "This is now bone of my bones, and flesh of my flesh."

A more contemporary translation of the
Hebrew would be a resounding "Whoopie! . . .
Where have you been all my life?"

Man and woman were designed by God so
that they are incomplete without each other.
That's why Moses said, " . . .a man shall
leave his father and his mother and shall cleave
to his wife and *they shall become one flesh*."
In searching for the secret of sex, hang on
to that one. Sexual expression is one of the key
ways a man and a woman become "one flesh."

But what is so unique about woman that
she is indispensible to man? There are two
ideas in the word Moses used: "helper"
and "suitable." The concept is that woman is
man's fundamentally perfect match—the
companion designed to provide for his whole-
ness, and he for hers. This basic fit was
created to satisfy individual longings in such
a way that when a man and woman are
united, they have the capacity to meet each
other's basic psychological and emotional
needs—to enable each other to become
fully human according to God's original
design.

One test of true love

If you're wondering whether the person you
are dating right now, or the man or woman
with whom you're in love, is right for you, ask
yourself, "Do I have a desire and capacity
to meet his or her real needs? Is this person

capable of more than merely satisfying my sexual urge, or raising my children, or bringing home the paycheck? Do we seem uniquely made to complement each other?" When you date, the search isn't just for someone you can *live with*. Instead, the real search should be for someone you *can't live without*.

In this book's first chapter, I mentioned that Paul Lewis and I met while dating twin sisters. I dated Paula for more than two years while I was going to graduate school. As our relationship grew, we became the best of friends. We enjoyed being with each other so much that falling in love was inevitable. Paula was an enormous encouragement to me. She supported me in my studies; she helped in my ministry; she shared my dreams and I shared hers. She had a wonderful sense of humor; she was attractive; she was everything I thought I had ever wanted in a wife. But as the relationship continued and we talked about marriage, doubt began to creep into both our minds. The perfect peace that God gives when things are right was missing. Ultimately, it became clear that we were not to marry each other. Breaking off that relationship was one of the most painful experiences of my life. But as perfect as the match was, Paula did not fill up all my empty places in the way that Dottie, my wife, now does. Dottie is

God's perfect complement for me. Paula wasn't.

It's interesting that Paul had a similar experience during college days. He dated Carolyn for nearly four years. Everyone assumed they would get married. The match was a great one. They enjoyed the same interests, worked together in student government and leadership positions, had the same goals for life. Their relationship was happy and fun. But, when it came time to make the final commitment to marriage, something wasn't right. Paul had no peace from God. Carolyn wasn't able to fill up all his empty places in the way that Leslie now does. And I'm not referring to sex. I'm talking about the way personalities, gifts, intellectual and emotional needs merge to make a total twenty-four-hour-a-day relationship.

The "one-flesh" relationship

Now when Moses said, "A man shall leave his father and his mother and shall cleave to his wife and they shall become one flesh," he used the strongest Hebrew words possible to describe this "leaving" and "cleaving." In leaving, the idea was to abandon and forsake the intimacy of the parent-child relationship, and to replace it with the intimacy of the husband-wife relationship. This new bond was to be as inseparable as the parent-child bond had been. Have you ever thought about how difficult it would be to become "unborn" from your natural parents? This is the concept behind the Hebrew word for "cleaving"—a separation-proof weld. And the evidence of that union, the continual reminder, was to be sexual intercourse, in which the man and woman become "one flesh."

Jesus affirmed this 1500 years later in a debate with the Jewish religious authorities. They were testing him on the subject of divorce. They were probing about the legal grounds on which a man could divorce a woman. And Jesus, knowing their motives, said, "Haven't you read . . . 'the two shall become one flesh?' Consequently, they are no more two, but one flesh. What therefore God has joined together, let no man separate."

And a little later, the Apostle Paul reinforced the principle. He was writing a letter to the people in the Christian church at Corinth. He was upset with what some of the deacons and elders were doing. Corinth was a city filled with heathen temples. In fact, their worship rituals probably made them one of the most "religious" cities in the world. In these temples, it was an act of worship to have sexual intercourse with the temple prostitutes.

Paul was angry because some of the Christian believers were reverting to their old ways and tripping off to the temple on Wednesday nights to "worship." And it wasn't to have a prayer meeting.

Paul wrote to them and said, "...do you not know that the one who joins himself to a harlot is one body with her? For He [Moses] says, 'The two will become one flesh.' " They become one unit in the same way as faith in Jesus Christ produces a bond between God's spirit and man's. In fact, God often uses the marriage relationship as an analogy to depict the union Christian believers have with him.

What is the real purpose of sex?

So what was in the mind of God the "Manufacturer," the one who designed sexuality, the one who created the male and female sex organs, when he created the urges and passions which lead to the sexual union? In the mind of this originator of sex, the basic purpose was to create unity. Sexual intercourse is intended to be a demonstration of the unity between a man and a woman.

"But wait a minute," you say. "I thought the Bible taught that the primary purpose for sex was procreation—childbearing." Isn't that right? No! That's the myth uninformed critics of Christianity have propagated to serve their own ends. Childbearing isn't the primary reason for sex. It's a secondary and very important reason, but it isn't the main reason God made sex.

The primary reason is the unity factor. It's to give a man and a woman "one-fleshness"— an experience in the physical realm which illustrates the intensity of the spiritual relationship a man or woman has with God when he or she is reborn through Jesus Christ.

This unity in sexual intercourse provides for a man and woman the most lasting enjoyment and maximum fulfillment they can possibly know. That's why sex at the right time, with the right person, in the right relationship is so incredibly perfect! And that's why the abuse of sex ultimately produces such enormous disappointment.

The misguided message

A lot of people have missed the message on what sex is all about. They've never heard it because of the erroneous caricatures that have been painted about the Christian view of sex. The Playboy philosophy, among many other voices, has led millions to believe that God is anti-sex, and that the Bible is negative on sexual enjoyment and fulfillment. They've asserted that to be a Christian believer, one would have to deny and repress his sexual urges.

Nothing could be further from the truth. In fact, some of the most beautiful words ever written about love between a man and a woman are found in the Bible, in the song of Solomon. Talk about two lovers, totally immersed in satisfying each other . . .the lovemaking poetry recorded there is incredible!

God isn't *against* sex. He's so *for* it that he wants every man and woman to understand how to get the most out of it. He wants them to realize it's not a casual toy; it's a fundamental pleasure to be carefully cherished, no matter how gratifying a "quick fix" might seem.

Sure, a lot of dumb things have been said about sex in the name of Christianity. And when you put these mistaken images together, you can create a very sorry looking caricature—a straw man. It may look like "the Christian view of sex," but it's not even close. And when you destroy this "straw man," as the Playboy philosophy has done, you really haven't destroyed anything. The facts are that sex is from God; he created it to fulfill and satisfy the deep urges he designed within every man and woman, and nothing will ever change the true facts.

When we stop long enough in our quest for maximum sexual expression, we will begin to realize how foolish it is to try to write our own "owner's manual." Only the original designer really knows how to make the sexual experience the ultimately satisfying expression we want it to be. When we finally wake up to these truths, we'll find what we've been searching for. We'll discover the secret.

Sex is more than a physical urge

Now, a lot of people say to me, "Come on, Josh, sex is just a physical act. Why, having intercourse is merely a physical thing, just the satisfying of a biological urge." Well, let me tell you, that may be true of your neighborhood tomcat. But because of the way God created it, sex for you and me involves all that we are. It's a complete sharing of ourselves, a complete vulnerability, a complete giving without holding anything back. That's what a maximum spiritual relationship with God is like. And sexual intercourse, being an illustration of that spiritual relationship, is like that, too. No matter how pleasurable, anything short of this complete sharing is not the maximum sexual experience God created for you and me.

I was speaking on this subject at Daytona Beach during Easter week. (And that can be rather exciting with all that flesh running around.) Whenever I speak on this subject, I usually irritate a few people —I guess I hit 'em where they sleep.

On this particular night, I really ticked off a guy. Oooh, he was mad. He came over to my motel room, banged on the door, and as I opened it, he pushed in and said, "I didn't agree with some of the things you said tonight." I said, "That's OK, it doesn't bother me." He said, "Well, I want to talk about it." I said, "I do, too." He said, "What's wrong with a meaningful physical relationship with a girl?" Ladies, you know that phrase "a lasting, meaningful relationship." One woman said, "Yeah, I had four of them last month."

Well, this guy said, "What's wrong with a lasting meaningful relationship with a girl if you love her, if you don't want to hurt anybody, and if you just want to enjoy yourselves? Why, I've had intercourse with twenty-six women." I said, "Wow, what a capacity for love. Tell me, Dave, when you get married, do you want to marry a woman that's been one of the twenty-five meaningful relationships of another guy?" He said, "No." Then I said, "Dave, you've nothing but a hypocrite. That's how meaningful sex is to you. You don't want someone to take from the woman you marry the same thing you are taking from these other women." You see, most guys don't like used furniture, but they love to be in the antiquing business.

Is sex the test of love?

Sex, as it was created by God, is very meaningful. It's not something you "get" or "do" or "have." Sexual expression grows and develops as a result of the permanent, ongoing, and maturing union between a man and a woman. It is evidence of the maximum oneness that God created it to express.

Some people use this as an argument for premarital sex. They say, "We'll have to have premarital sex to see if we're compatible." Boy, you sure would have to have a lot of it, because the problem of compatibility is not physical. The physical relationship almost always works. The problem of compatibility is the problem of ultimate oneness —complementing each other in a way that makes for a giving and full personhood. And that involves the totality of who you are, your spiritual (God-sensitive) and soulish (man-sensitive) as well as physical dimensions. In God's design, the more spiritual and soulish unity a couple has, the better their sex life will be as it grows, matures, and develops over a period of time.

At a college on the West Coast, there's a Christian professor who is eighty-four years old. One day in a sociology class a coed asked him, "Tell me, sir, when do you stop enjoying sex?" He replied, "I don't know, but it's sometime after eighty-four." And that's the way it was created to be. Sex is meant always to be growing, maturing, and developing into maximum unity and ultimate oneness.

This kind of unity, enjoyment, and oneness can never be achieved by a "one-night stand." In fact, it can't really grow outside a marriage commitment that is final and permanent.

Sexuality originated in the creative act of God which put man on the face of this earth. You can choose not to believe this. You can decide instead that human sexuality is a mere biological function no different from the sexual attractions of two dogs running loose in the park. You can experiment and play all the mental and social games you want. But any other scheme or function for sexuality besides the one God had in mind is doomed to fall short of fulfilling the corresponding need and sexual longing God put within you. Sex is like any other process; it succeeds only when you follow the manufacturer's directions.

And for all its apparent staying power and lasting attraction, sex is fragile. It takes time and needs security. It only really blossoms when enjoyed in the context of genuine unconditional love. In fact, you'll never discover ultimate sex until you have understood how to give and receive ultimate love.

It is often said, if you love someone, you'll

express it sexually. The truth is, if you can't express your love apart from sex, it's not true love. So let's examine this true love. What is it like?

4
WHAT'S TRUE LOVE LIKE?
♥

If you gave me only twelve minutes to speak to a psychology class on maximum sex, I would talk about love. Because what you decide love is—the attitudes you have about it, how you express it, and how you respond to all the psychological games played in our society in the name of love—all of this will determine whether you will ever find the sexual fulfillment you want. What my wife and I enjoy in our marriage, I believe, is the result of what we both prepared for as single persons.

A few years ago, a lot of people called me prudish. They thought I was out of date. They said my ideas about sex and marriage were old-fashioned. But now, many of them would give anything to reap the benefits I'm harvesting from the attitudes about love I developed as a single person. The familiar saying is: "You are what you have been becoming." And nowhere is this more true than in the area of love and sex. The patterns of loving you practice now will determine the quality of love you will experience later.

Three kinds of love

If you're feeling a bit confused about love it's probably because you're unaware that there are really three kinds of love. As I describe them to you, I want to use them as a mirror to evaluate the love relationships you now have with your friends, family, and members of the opposite sex.

The first type of love is the only kind many people have ever known. It's what I call "love, IF." It's the love you and I give or receive when certain requirements are met. You have to do something to earn it. "If you are a good child, Daddy will give you his love." "If you meet my expectations as a lover . . . if you will satisfy my desires . . . if you will go to bed with me, I will love you." Parents often communicate this type of love by saying, in effect, to their children, "If you'll get good grades . . . if you'll choose a different set of friends . . . if you'll dress or act a certain way, you'll have our love." The love is offered in exchange for something the lover wants. Its motivation is basically selfish. Its purpose is to gain something in exchange for love.

I've met so many women who know no

other type of love than the one which says,
"I will love you if you will put out." What
they don't realize is that the love they
expect to win from someone by meeting his
sexual demands is a cheap love which
can't satisfy and which is never worth the
price. This type of love is demonstrated by a
graduate student who said to me, "Why
should I want love when I can have sex? Love
is surrender. Sex is conquest."

"Love, *if*" always has strings attached. As
long as the conditions are met, things are
fine. When there is reluctance—to have sex,
to get an abortion—the love ceases to
flow. Sadly, this kind of conditional love
almost always destroys itself because, sooner
or later, one partner will fail to meet the
requirements of the other.

Many marriages break up because they
were built on this kind of love. The husband
or wife turns out to be in love, not with
the actual personality of the spouse, but rather
with some imaginary, glorified, romanticized
image. When disillusionment sets in, or the
expectations cease to be met, "love, *if*" often
turns into resentment, and tragically, the
persons involved may never know why.

Less than the best
The second type of love (and I think most
people marry on the basis of this one), is
"love, *BECAUSE OF*." In this love, the
person is loved because of something he is,

something he has, or something he does. In other words, the love is produced by a certain condition or quality in the loved person's life.

"Love, *because of*" often sounds like this: "I love you because you are pretty," "I love you because you're rich," "I love you because you give me security," "I love you because you're so different from the others, so popular, or so famous, etc." For example, you may know a woman who loves a particular guy because he is a super athlete. She just can't imagine herself settling for anything less than No. 1. It really doesn't matter much which particular fellow is the athlete. She isn't really in love with him; she is in love with his position, his status, and his popularity.

Often, someone will say to me, " 'Love, *because of*' sounds pretty good to me. I want to be loved for what I am, for the qualities and things in my life. What's wrong with that?" Nothing, perhaps. All of us want to be loved for something in our life. And it's certainly preferable to the "love, *if*" kind of love. The "if" kind of love has to be earned, and requires a lot of effort. Having someone love us because of what we are puts us more at ease. We know there is something about us which is lovable.

To be loved this way, however, soon becomes no better than trying to earn the "if" kind of love. And it's a shaky foundation upon which to establish a marriage or any lasting relationship.

Consider, for example, the problem of competition. What happens when someone comes along with more of the quality for which you are loved? Suppose you're a woman, and your beauty is one of the hallmarks of your husband's love. What happens when a more beautiful woman comes on the scene?

If the love of your girl friend or wife is based on your salary, or the things and experiences it can buy, what happens if you lose your job, or become disabled, or for whatever reasons become unable to earn the salary you used to? Or, what happens when someone with more money or more earning power comes on the scene? Will the competition put you on edge? Will it threaten your love? If it will, then yours is a "love, *because of*" type of love.

And there's another problem with "*because of*" love. It's found in the fact that most of us are two types of people. There's the person on the outside, the Josh McDowell or the Paul Lewis that meets the eye of the public. And then there's the other side of us, that deep-down-inside person that few, if anyone, really knows. What I've learned from counseling people who have "love, *because of*" relationships is that one or both partners are truly afraid to let the other know what they're really like deep down inside. They're fearful that, if the truth were known, they would be less accepted, or less loved, or maybe rejected altogether.

Is there anything in your life that you cannot share with your partner out of fear of even minor discomfort or rejection? If so, you'll have a difficult time experiencing maximum sex, because profound sexual intimacy requires 100 percent trust and giving. If there's any insecurity in your love, if there's any fear, the first place it will be manifested is between the sheets; because in a maximum expression of true sexuality, we become completely vulnerable—we're wide open to the other individual. It is this very openness that makes possible maximum sexual gratification and sharing, and this same openness allows for the deepest sort of hurt if we're not completely accepted. So, in a "love, *because of*" relationship, you can never totally give of yourself in sharing physical love, because the risk of being hurt is so great.

I was sharing this with a student audience on the East Coast when one of the women listening broke out crying. She was beautiful —engaged to be married. In a car accident, one side of her face had become terribly scarred. Plastic surgery had been required to make repairs, but her relationship was

a "love, *because of*" relationship. Fear immediately entered her thinking and the entire
relationship deteriorated. It was a classic case
of "love, *because of*." It was reflected
in the phrase, "I love you, and I want you
because. . . ." Much of the love we know in
our lives is of this kind, leaving us very
uncertain of its permanence.

Love without conditions

Thankfully, there is yet another kind of
love. A love so startling and so beautiful that
I wish everyone could bend his will to
accept it. It is love without conditions.

This love says, "I love you in spite of what
you may be like deep down inside. I love
you no matter what could change about you.
You can't do anything to turn off my love.
I love you, PERIOD!"

"Love, *period*" isn't a blind love. Far from
it. It can know a great deal about the
other person. It can know the person's short-
comings. It knows the other's faults, yet
it totally accepts that individual without
demanding anything in return. There's
no way you can earn this type of love. You
can't do anything to increase it. You
can't turn it off. It has no strings attached. It
is different from "because of" love in
that it isn't produced by some attractive
quality in the person who is being loved. This
kind of love would love even the most

worthless individual as if he were of infinite value.

"Love, *period*" can only be experienced by a complete and fulfilled individual—one who doesn't have to constantly take from life's relationships to fill the voids in his or her own life. A fulfilled person is truly free to give in a relationship without demanding anything in return.

Whether you realize it or not, "love, *period*" is more important to you than anything else. If you are not presently experiencing this kind of love, it is likely that you are still hoping that someday you will, or you are clinging to a treasured memory of a time in the past when you were loved in this way. Life without something resembling this type of love will eventually lead to despair. "Love, *period*" is a giving relationship. It can't wait to *give*. The other two kinds of love can't wait to *get*. GIVE is how you spell "love, *period*." It's freely giving of yourself. And in this relationship, there's no room for fear, frustration, pressure, envy, or jealousy.

A new motivation for performance

When my wife, Dottie, and I were engaged, she wrote me a letter. And in it she said, "Honey, I know that you accept me just the way I am. I don't have to perform for you. I don't have to do or be any certain thing . . .you just love me." And then she added, "Do you know what that does for me? It just causes in me a greater desire to be more of a woman for you."

At this point, a lot of guys will say, "Hey, if I loved my girl in spite of the way she looks, in spite of the way she does things, she'd just let herself go to pot." No she wouldn't. Because "love, *period*" is a giving love. It is actually God's love poured through an individual, and it's so winsome, so irresistible that it draws out the best in the other person. It causes creative changes in the other person. The changes aren't demanded, they are simply a natural response to unconditional love.

My wife loves me so much that I don't have to perform for her. Her unstoppable love triggers in me a natural desire to be the type of person she knows I ought to be. I don't have to be that way, I just want to. It's the natural response to her "love, *period*" kind of love for me.

This is what divine love is all about. God, speaking through the ancient prophet Jeremiah, says, "I have loved you with an everlasting love; therefore I have drawn you with lovingkindness." You see, God loved me even when I didn't believe he had anything to say about my life. He loved me in spite of my sins. And the curious thing is that it triggered in me the natural response. I responded to his love. That's the real truth that led me to become a Christian.

I was speaking on sex, love, and dating at Purdue University when a student from Germany stood up. He had the Kinsey Report in his hand. (Of course, it's a little out of date.) But he stood up and said, "Look, McDowell, we want facts, not all this philosophizing about love. We want facts. The Kinsey Report is factual and secular, and it recommends that girls have various premarital sexual experiences in order to have proper adjustment in marriage."

Well, that sounded pretty good to most of the men in the room, and it deserved a straightforward response. I said, "You might be right, but did you read why? In *Sexual Behavior in the Human Female,* he points out that it is common knowledge that many girls do not have pleasant sexual experiences the first few times. It often takes several weeks, months, or even a year to make the adjustments and to totally relax and enjoy sex completely. And then Dr. Kinsey goes on and shows the kind of love many men have for their wives. He says the majority of the men will not be patient with their wives in this area. Therefore, he recommends that women have various premarital experiences with various guys because the man that supposedly loves her will not be patient with her."

I can't think of a more depraved reason
for doing something. I hope you women
will do yourself a favor and wait for that guy
to come along who loves you for who
you are with a giving love. Who says, "I love
you, *period*." Who won't rob you of the
opportunity to express your love for each other
in marriage, but will be patient enough
for you to make the necessary adjustments
together. There isn't another area in
which a guy can better demonstrate his love
for his wife than by being patient and
tender in the area of sexual adjustments.

The choice is yours

Which of the three kinds of love would you
like to have? Very few people purpose-
fully choose the "if" kind of love. It requires
a continual and endless effort to perform.
So, two other loves remain. And surprisingly,
many people choose love "because of."
Perhaps it's more flattering to be loved this
way. Being loved for something you are or
have is satisfying. It builds your own opinion
of yourself. But it is a fragile fabrication
and ultimately self-defeating.

The secret of loving is the third type of love:
"love, *period*." It's not too common,
because the only lasting source of this love is
God himself. No individual can consistently
display this kind of love without God's Holy
Spirit indwelling and controlling him.

And God freely implants this love at the very
center of any individual who is willing
to admit that he wants it, and that he needs
God's help to love in this way.

Why is this love so scarce? Why is it such a
secret? Because it runs cross-grain with
man's pride. We don't like to admit that we
can't be whatever we want to be by sheer
willpower and determination alone. And we'd
rather ignore this "love, *period*" kind
of love because when it comes to sex, it
requires discipline and self-control. It requires
that we put our emotions and physical
urges on notice that they serve us; we do not
serve them.

Are you tired of "love, *if*" and "love,
because of"? You can have "love, *period*." It's
the secret of loving. And if you want to
begin experiencing it in your relationships
with the opposite sex, it will probably
involve some adjustment in your thinking.
You'll need to reeducate your most important
sex organ.

5
WHAT IS YOUR MOST IMPORTANT SEX ORGAN?
♥

Whenever I speak on the Christian view of love and sex, it is not uncommon for one or two students to come up to me and say, "Just a minute, having sex is a mere physical act. Why, it's no different from drinking a glass of water." Well, let me tell you, there's a lot of difference between sex and drinking a glass of water. Whether exploitative or nonexploitative, sex involves all that you are as an individual. Sex is never merely a physical act. As we said earlier, the physical aspect of sex almost always works. Any malfunction is usually in your mind. Your mind is your most important sex organ!

By now, I hope you're beginning to understand that sex was designed by God as a vehicle for enjoyment and for the expression

of ultimate unity and oneness between
a man and a woman within the bonds of a
permanent and lasting relationship. I
hope you're beginning to see that casual sex
can never be ultimately fulfilling or
satisfying; that whatever gratification one
may experience on a one-night stand, or
even in a series of longer relationships, it only
serves to dilute the possibility of robust
and satisfying love. Yet all of this is exactly
opposite to what society is constantly
telling us.

You and I are being continually bombarded
by messages and pressures based on a
sexual ethic and practice which is false and
incomplete. When Kinsey questioned
women about their sex lives in the 1940s, he
found that one-half to two-thirds of
married women reported having regular or
frequent orgasms. Thirty years later,
a survey of women has revealed that three-
fourths of American women "always or
nearly always" have an orgasm during intercourse. The number of women achieving
physical satisfaction has increased substan-
tially. In view of this, Jody Gaylin
Heyward, writing in the May 1978 *Ladies
Home Journal,* asks, "Why, then, are women
going to sexual dysfunction clinics in
record numbers? And why are there so many
stories of disappointment and disenchant-
ment from therapists who are treating

women of all ages? Maybe because there is
more to being satisfied than mere physical
pleasure. Maybe because frequency of
orgasm doesn't meaure psychological fulfillment."

Sex in three dimensions

Jody's right. Let's look at why sex is so
often unfulfilling, even within marriage. It's
because sex, as God created it, involves
oneness on three levels—three different
dimensions. If one of these three dimensions
is missing, you are going to experience
a diluted relationship.

The first dimension is obvious. It's the
physical dimension. It's the one in which two
people become one physically. A basic
biological union.

The second dimension is the soulish
dimension. In it, the real you as a person, as
a being with ideas, desires, and feelings,
becomes one with another person.

The third dimension is the spiritual
dimension, the one in which two people
become one spiritually. Sex is a three-
dimensional act, and if one of these three
dimensions is missing, you will always
experience a watered-down relationship and
less than maximum fulfillment.

Most of us grow up unaware of these three
crucial dimensions. We begin loving with the
attitude that, "If I'm good at sex, if I

can really please my partner physically, it doesn't matter what other problems we have. We'll be able to overcome them." This is one of the biggest lies propagated today. A good sex life very seldom produces a good relationship. But I know one thing: a good marriage produces a fantastic sex life, because good sex is the result of a good relationship rather than the cause of it. Yet most people are striving to find real unity through physical sex alone.

Can sex solve a problem?

Let me give you an example of how some guys think. A problem develops in his relationship with a woman, and the first thing the guy wants to do is go to bed. Why? Because he believes, "If I can please my mate physically, the problem, no matter what it is, will take care of itself." Usually, the woman doesn't want the man to touch her until the problem is talked out. Sex is the last thing she wants. That doesn't deter a lot of men, however. And they begin to pressure the woman until she gives in. As a result, she develops negative attitudes toward sex.

This is why I stress the fact that unless you develop the spiritual and soulish dimensions of your lives, you're going to rob yourself and your mate in the area of your physical relationship.

How important, then, is the physical

dimension? I think it's very important. But I
believe in a maximum relationship. The
physical dimension only makes up about one-
twelfth of a marriage relationship. But
it's a great one-twelfth! However, it must be
kept in perspective. That's why your
mind is your most important sexual organ! I
know many couples who have destroyed
beautiful relationships because they have
programmed false facts and attitudes
about sex into their minds.

In preparing for this book, my wife and I
gathered information from a number of
reliable sources—people who constantly
counsel and conduct research in the area of sex
and marriage. Many of these sources
point out that as high as 85 to 90 percent of
problems that appear to be sex-related
are really problems in the soulish and spiritual
dimensions of life. Because the physical
dimension is the most tangible part of a
relationship, it's often the place where
problems show up first.

When I say this, some people become
critical and defensive. And it's these same
people who tell me sex is like "a drink
of water." They come up after a lecture and
say, "Josh, not all sex is meaningful.
With some people it is; with others, it's not."
I think that attitude is totally in error.
Every time you have a physical encounter,
from heavy petting on, it is meaningful. It

involves all that you are as an individual, including your mind.

Programming for success...

And what is this problem with our minds? The difficulty is that many of us have been programmed incorrectly. We've been bombarded with misinformation. We've been told that the key to sexual fulfillment is to join the revolution; to cast off the old morality and to enjoy the new; to experiment with a variety of partners; to move around and have your needs met. Discipline is out. Gratification is in.

In computer talk, it's like the familiar adage of "garbage in, garbage out." If we've been programmed (or allowed ourselves to be programmed) with incorrect information, we're going to form incorrect conclusions. And that's what many of us have done. We have emphasized the physical instead of the mental. And to rediscover fulfilling love and satisfying sex, we have some reprogramming to do.

When I was speaking at Stanford University, I had the opportunity to interview a tremendous man, Dr. Gerhard Dirks. He is one of the men who helped develop the computer. I read that Einstein had an I.Q. of around 207. Dirk's is 206! He's a brilliant mind and, at the time, he held more patents for IBM than any other man alive.

During a four-and-a-half-hour conversation, he shared with me how the computer was developed from the human body. It was thrilling. We talked about how the human body and mind are programmed. And I discovered that programming takes place in three ways: (1) visually (by what it sees), (2) audibly (by what it hears), and (3) mechanically (by what it does). I asked Dr. Dirks to tell me specifically how the human body and mind are programmed in the area of sex. He shared his own convictions on the subject.

When a girl has intercourse with one fellow, he said, that man programs her to respond visually, audibly, and mechanically to a certain set of actions. Dr. Dirks continued, "I believe what happens is this: A girl is programmed by one or two guys (or twenty). Then she meets the man that she marries and she cannot totally respond to his programming because of the conflicting programming of prior experiences." And then he added, "I really believe that for maximum sex, it's best for two people to be programmed together."

What programs you?

Dr. Dirks then brought in the male perspective. When a guy has a sexual experience, he never forgets it. It's programmed directly into the mind. Women are basically programmed by touch. A guy is programmed by eyesight. While women are aroused or stimulated principally through touch, all a man has to do is see. A woman is turned on physically through caressing. All a guy has to do is look...and BOOM, he's ready at 110 percent capacity.

This is why your mind is so important—the most important sexual organ you have. And how you program your mind becomes critical. We men need to be especially careful of what we look at. Women need to be careful of what they wear and how they are touched. And I realize that in the context of the society in which we live and love, what I'm saying borders on the absurd. But if the way you program your mind directly affects your potential for sexual fulfillment, taking precautions is well worth the effort.

A lot of men and women are very casual about what they see or how they are touched. As a result, they numb the very sensorial areas God created to arouse and fulfill them sexually. To express his attitude of freedom and liberation, a guy may surround himself with pin-ups and lots of visual stimuli. He may frequent sexually stimulating movies. The long-term result will be a loss of sensitivity to the very things which God designed to fulfill him within

the security of the marriage relationship.
Because of this loss, it will constantly take
more and more intense sexual stimulation
to produce the same degree of arousal.

If a woman allows and encourages men to
touch and fondle her in a casual manner,
she, too, programs herself for a diluted
response to the man to whom she will one day
want to give herself most completely.

And just to show you the positive side of
this programming principle, consider
the effect upon a man and woman within
marriage.

If a man's initial programming is with his
wife, and hers with her husband, the
first lovemaking encounter provides an initial
burst of data and pleasure response in
both of them. Those patterns of initiation and
response are filed away in their minds.
Their next sexual encounter adds to it and
expands it further. And the hundreds of
subsequent experiences of life, interaction,
and the physical sharing of love continue
to build and further refine their mental
programs.

It's not hard to understand, then, why sex
within marriage doesn't become boring,
but rather more and more satisfying over an
entire lifetime. When properly programmed,
our minds are an incredible organ for
sexual fulfillment.

You can be reprogrammed!

To experience for ourselves the maximum fulfillment in love and sexuality, most of us are going to need some rather dramatic and serious reprogramming. And I think I can speak confidently about this because I wasn't reprogrammed until I was a student at Kellogg College.

While a student, I set out to destroy Christianity. I thought it was a big farce and I wanted others to be as aware of this travesty as I was. But as I tried, I could not intellectually refute Christian truth. And as a result of intensive investigation, I came to the conclusion that Jesus Christ was who he claimed to be—the Son of God, the Messiah.

And so in 1959, during my second year at the university, I trusted Christ as my Savior and Lord. I invited him to come into my life. And he began to change my mind and my thought forms. Within a year and a half, he fulfilled me from the inside out. In fact, he so renewed and changed me that my sexual perspective changed. He made it possible for me to truly "give" in a relationship without demanding something in return. That's when I learned the basic difference between "love, *if*" and "love, *because of*" on one hand, and "I love you, *period*" on the other.

I firmly believe that this is step one in mind and life renewal—letting Christ begin to remake you. And when you're in the process of renewal—when your life is under construction—I think it means you exert a little discipline in your approach to members of the opposite sex.

I get so tired of the lines I hear used on campus. "If you love me, you'll let me." Or, "But I can't help myself." When you hear those or use them yourself, remember it's strictly "love, *if*" or "love, *because of*."

Then, of course, there's the old standby, "Everyone's doing it." What a wishy-washy reason for doing something—just because someone else does it. I'm so glad that Jesus Christ gave me a new character and the capacity to avoid doing something just because it's popular or someone else is doing it.

And, finally, there's the old standard, "But just this once?" I've seen so many long-standing "just this once" relationships, I've lost count. All of these "lines" and motivations are based on a very cheap, conditional type of love. Renewal of the mind begins with Jesus Christ and continues by exchanging our lines and approaches for "love, *period*" relationships.

Why wait until marriage?

Whenever I begin to talk about mind renewal and Jesus Christ, someone will always say, "What's the big deal? Why should

I wait for the right time and the right person? Why do you feel God wants sex to be reserved for marriage? What if you're in love and committed to each other but you just haven't gone through the formal procedure of a wedding ceremony?"

My answer is this: God designed sex and he has a lot to say about it. One of the things he says in the Bible is to "flee fornication." Fornication is the biblical word for premarital sex—any sex outside of marriage. When I first heard this, before I became a Christian, I was irked. I felt like saying, "Who do you think you are, God or something?" And later I discovered that is exactly who he is.

But the more I studied this instruction, the more I talked to young people, and the more I reflected on Scripture and personal experience, the more I became convinced that every time God gives a negative commandment in the Bible, there are always two positive motives behind it. The first is for our protection. The second is for our provision. In essence, God was saying to me, "Josh, wait. Because I love you so much, I'm going to protect you and provide for you so that you can have a maximum relationship with your wife-to-be."

But why wait? I think one reason is to build self-control; something all of us need a little more of. There are many times *after*

you're married when you *cannot* have
sex due to illness, separation, or some stages
of pregnancy. When you learn to control
your sex life before marriage, you can control
it afterwards. And this self-control adds
the factor of trust to a relationship.

If my wife knows that I was able to control
my sex life before marriage, it builds
trust in her mind and strengthens our relationship when I'm on the road traveling.
You say, "Oh, that's childish." Maybe it is,
but it gives us and our marriage an advantage.
Because of the way God designed sex,
it requires a total abandonment of yourself
to the other person. And that requires
100 percent trust. When there's distrust in a
relationship, you're in trouble. Discipline
before marriage makes possible maximum sex
and love later.

Getting back to square one

About now, a lot of people say, "Josh, I
want to wait for the right time and right
relationship for sex. But how can I do it?"
Others add, "You know, I haven't waited
in my physical relationship, but from now on
I want to wait. How do I explain it to
my boyfriend when we've been having sex?"

I'm the first to admit that stopping after
you've started is a real problem. It's
just plain tough to give it up. But I think it's
necessary to do so. And while my answer

to these questions is *simple,* it's not *easy.* I suggest that you tell your lover a simple, direct "No," and explain your reasons. If he (or she) persists, he doesn't really love you. What has been represented as love was really only a desire for sexual release. I don't care if it's a man pushing a woman or a woman pushing a man's standard in this area. I believe that anyone who seeks to compromise you in one area has the capacity to attempt to compromise your standards or desires in other areas. The area may be lying, cheating, or whatever. And this type of individual is not good marriage material. Remember, marriage is where maximum sex and love take place. I wouldn't want someone with a compromising approach to be the father or mother of my children.

Some practical suggestions

Now if you want to positively program your mind, I'll give some practical ideas. In addition to the essential basis of a vital relationship with Jesus Christ, and being careful of the "lines" you use or respond to, here are other steps you can take.

Over 2700 years ago, the writer of Proverbs wrote of man, "For as he thinks within himself, so he is." (And by the way, that applies to women, too.) The point is: what you *think about* determines who you are.

Thoughts ⟶ attitudes ⟶ actions ⟶ accomplishments is the sequence. And 750 years later, Paul, under God's inspiration, added these words, "Do not be conformed to this world but be transformed by the *renewing of your mind*." The principle, then, is: what you think, you become. The way to change your actions is to renew your mind.

I mentioned earlier the computer phrase, "garbage in, garbage out." Let's get specific. Watch what you *read*. You know what's good for you and what's not. If there's a certain magazine or book that causes you to fantasize erotically, it would be best to leave that book or magazine alone. Erotic fantasies can cause unrealistic expectations which may never be fulfilled later in marriage.

If you find the films you're attending are slowly (or quickly) working away at your newfound convictions, you may have to stop attending them. You're not dumb. You know what affects you. You have to make the decision. I can't give you some iron-clad standards that will accurately satisfy your requirements. But I can say, "as a person thinks, so is he." And I can unequivocally say that we all need to be transformed by the renewal of our minds through Jesus Christ.

Another crucial area for renewal is your *speech*. What you say has almost as great an effect on what you do as what you think.

If you are constantly involved with off-color jokes, sexual innuendoes, and provocative talk, it's going to influence you and those around you. I'm certainly not saying it's wrong to talk about sex, but be careful of the context. Are you simply rephrasing society's view that sex is a game—a "playful business"? Or is your talk reinforcing the beauty, importance, and values of a total person relationship and maximum sex within maximum marriage?

And finally, watch your dating patterns. Once you've crossed a certain point physically, it's hard to return. So decide in advance how much sexual stimulation you and your partner will give one another. And beware of the setting. Regardless of how "renewed" your mind is, lying on the plush carpet of a van listening to music at 2:00 A.M. is plain stupidity if you're serious about the sanctity of sex.

But "no-no's" are only half the answer. You need to refill the areas of your mind you've emptied. Renewal involves reprogramming.

The psalmist had a suggestion that holds true today, "How can a young person keep his way pure? By guarding it according to thy Word." I'm a firm believer in the importance of *Bible study.* Feeding on God's Word will counteract all the programming you get from the world's system. (I suggest if you haven't done much Bible reading before, you find a modern translation of Scripture and begin to read. Start in the Gospel of John in the New Testament; later read the Old Testament.) You'll find by responding obediently to God's Word, your life will take on unbelievable meaning and some of the emptiness you formerly tried to fill with sexual activity will be filled with God's own love for you. That's mind renewal. After all, your mind is your most important sex organ.

6
CAN I HAVE A FRESH START?

♥

About this point, you've likely formed one
of three opinions concerning what I've
said about sex and loving. You're either
saying, "Josh, you're right on. I agree and I've
been trying to live and love the way you
have described." Or you are saying, "Josh,
you're out of your mind—a reject from
the eighteenth century. I'm going to live the
way twentieth-century people do."

Still others of you are saying,"It's pretty
new to me, but the message makes sense.
My life style doesn't even come close to what
you have described. At times, I've felt a
bit uneasy about some of my sexual patterns;
sometimes I've felt like a loser. Now I
feel downright guilty. I want a new life. I
want to clean up my act, sexually. I'd

like to have "love, *period,*" but I don't know where the change should start."

Since those of you in the first category already understand the secret of loving, and you who are in the second category aren't interested, I'd like to talk for a moment to everyone who has responded the third way. And let me say at the outset, there is enormous hope. You *can* change and have the kind of life you want. Here's how.

Some of you in this group are not Christian believers. I'll address you first. And then I want to talk to you who are Christians but still find yourself a long way from the mark. I've met hundreds, and heard from thousands of you who have deep guilt about your sexual behavior.

A fresh start begins here

If you are one who does not yet have a personal relationship with Jesus Christ, the answer to your guilt feelings is not a long list of sexual taboos. Nor is the answer found in saying, "Free sex for you is fine." I think the real starting point for you and everyone else is where it was for me in 1959 —the discovery of Jesus Christ. That's right, a personal life-changing encounter with the exciting person of Jesus Christ. Now, before you tune me out, let me give you two basic reasons why.

First is the area of forgiveness—the cleansing of the conscience. I believe one of the first steps toward control in the area of sex (or any area for that matter) is the experience of forgiveness and the removal of guilt. God is in the forgiving business. One of the major reasons Jesus invaded earth was to forgive men and cleanse their consciences. That's why the Bible says, "Though your sins are as scarlet, they will be as white as snow. . . ." That's the primary reason Jesus Christ died on the cross—to forgive you; to forgive me; to forgive us. We are all in need of forgiveness.

The director of a mental institution said in a seminar that 50 percent of his patients could go home if they knew they were forgiven. When Dr. Billy Graham was lecturing in Honolulu, a group of psychologists were sent there to criticize his talk. They could only agree unanimously on one thing: When Dr. Graham called for people to repent and receive God's forgiveness through Christ, it was a psychologically sound move because people needed to be forgiven.

Do you know why people *feel* guilty? Because they *are* guilty. The Bible points out that all of us have sinned and fallen short of God's glory. "All" includes you and me. And if you come to Jesus right now and ask him to become your Lord and Savior

(giving him authority to direct your life),
Jesus Christ will immediately forgive
you and cleanse your conscience.

When I told one student this, he replied,
"How do you know God will forgive me?
You don't even know what I've done." I said,
"Mister, I don't care what you've done,
I don't care how gross you've been. God loves
you and he will forgive you and wipe the
slate clean."

How can I know this? What gives me this
confidence? First, it's written down in God's
book, the Bible. And God doesn't lie.
For an enormous number of reasons, I have
confidence in his Word. Second, I distinctly
remember that night in the university
when I confessed Christ as Savior; I went to
bed that night and slept like a baby. And
not once since then has guilt ever kept me
awake.

Freedom without bondage
The second reason why I think it's
important that you turn to Christ is the whole
area of freedom. Real freedom. Jesus
Christ has the power to set us free. You see,
the Christian life is a supernatural life.
According to Scripture and according to my
experiences and those of millions of other
Christians throughout history, when someone
trusts Christ, the Holy Spirit enters into
a person's life in a supernatural way and begins

to change that person from the inside
out. You are literally "under construction."

And this freedom that Christ gives is
completely different from the world's idea of
freedom. The world tells us we're free
in sex through indulgence. Jesus makes a lot
more sense. He says, "You're free in sex
through control." With Christ, we *can*
control this area of our lives. And until we can
control it, we're never really free. We
are in bondage to our passions.

The reason so many people have to espouse
free sex is that they seemingly have no other
choice. They can't control themselves.
But if you come to Christ and confess him as
Savior and Lord, he'll forgive you, cleanse
you, enter into your life, and change you on
the inside in much the same way that
he changed me. He will give you the capacity
to say "no" in areas of your life in which
you need to say "no," and "yes" in areas of
your life that require a "yes."

I've described this dynamic relationship
with Jesus Christ, but I haven't really told you
how to begin such a relationship with
him. You might be saying, "I didn't know
that Christianity was a relationship with
Jesus Christ. I'd like to know Christ
personally. I'd like to know that I'm forgiven;
that my conscience is cleansed. I'd like
to know for sure that Jesus Christ lives in me."

I remember when I had that attitude

and didn't know what to do. A friend of mine said, "Josh, I'll pray the prayer that I prayed to trust Christ and maybe my words will help you to express to God your desire to trust Christ." And ever since Jerry did that for me, I've been so appreciative I've wanted to do it for other people.

So, I'll share with you what Jerry shared with me. If you want to pray it where you are right now, I encourage you to do so. And as you pray, remember that God says in John 1:12, "But as many as received Him, to them He gave the right to become children of God."

This is the prayer that I prayed:

Lord Jesus, I need you. Forgive me and cleanse me. Right this moment I trust you as Savior and Lord. Take over the throne of my life; change me from the inside out. Thank you that I can trust you. In Christ's name, Amen.

It's not the most complicated prayer you've ever heard. But it is the most significant. With that prayer, you can begin a permanent new relationship with God.

Nurturing your fresh start
If you just prayed that prayer, I'd like to suggest that you read the third chapter of the book of John three times before you go

to bed tonight. And before you read it,
pray a prayer something like this, "God, if
you are God and Christ is your Son, and
if what I read in this Book is true and you
really did come into my life in response
to the request I just made and you forgave me,
please give me the conviction of it. Help
me to know internally that it's true." Then
read John, chapter three, three times. In
the following days and months, look for
changes in your life in two areas—attitudes
and actions.

When a fundamental change has happened
at the very center of your being, it's
only natural that it will begin to show in
various ways. Often, there is a rather
immediate sense of new inner peace—that
insecure feeling is replaced with a sense
of calm security. You'll find yourself
beginning to respond to life's circumstances
in new ways. Things that usually frighten
or anger you may no longer do so. You will
begin to express a more selfless love than
you've ever had before.

There may be other changes in attitude or
actions which will be uniquely given by
God to you. To gain insight and understanding of your new life, read the rest of John
in your Bible, and also look for a group
of Christians with which you can communicate and learn more about your new faith.

Christians have problems, too

Now let me address myself to Christians —you who have previously invited Christ into your lives. Strange as it may seem, Christians can have more problems in the area of sexual control than non-Christians.

As I've said before, sex involves the physical, soulish, and spiritual parts of us. Therefore, when a Christian man and woman enter into a close personal relationship, they begin with a common spiritual bond. And if their personalities integrate easily, there will be a natural tendency to progress into the physical area. Unless they realize this, it can be very difficult to control.

Charlie Shedd, who has often written on this subject, facetiously says, "I wouldn't encourage dating couples to pray together. Good prayer leads to good sex." And he's right—with the right person, in the right situation (marriage), sex is good and gorgeous. And so is prayer. I'm a firm believer in the truth that the stronger your spiritual bond is, the stronger your bond can be sexually.

Several months ago, a national magazine did a survey of religious men and women and concluded that "religious conviction adds to sexual enjoyment." They discovered that where there were strong religious convictions, there was greater enjoyment sexually. I think the primary reason for this parallel between religious conviction and enjoyable sex is that Jesus teaches that people are of value. You don't use people. You think first of what you can *give to* them rather than what you can *get from* them. And in marriage, this attitude of giving rather than getting eliminates many sexual problems. Before marriage, it can lead to a few problems because "love, *period*" is so winsome, people naturally gravitate toward greater physical involvement.

Now, if you are a Christian who has failed in the area of sexual control and feels guilty, let me tell you how to lose that guilt forever.

Step one is confession. Forgiveness for a Christian is as important as forgiveness for a non-Christian. When Jesus Christ died on that cross almost 2,000 years ago, he died for every sin you ever committed or ever will commit—past, present, or future. You may say, "Wait a minute, what about my future sins?" Well, 2,000 years ago, all your sins were future. But Christ died for you.

"So if they've been forgiven," you may ask, "why should I confess them?" I think there are two reasons. One, the Bible tells us to. In 1 John, the Apostle John writes to Christians, "If we confess our sins, He is faithful and righteous to forgive us our sins and to cleanse us from all unrighteousness."

The second reason is personal and pragmatic. I encourage believers to confess so they can start experiencing what they already have—forgiveness. So many Christians run around like they've been paroled, when in reality they've been pardoned. And they don't realize the difference between the two. When you're on parole, you check in with your parole officer regularly. The crime is still on record. You have a list of restrictions for your life. You live life under constraint, constantly on guard, wondering if you're doing something wrong. When you're pardoned, you're totally free. No restrictions. No parole officer. It's as if the crime had not been committed.

For an even better understanding of pardon, let's look at the Greek word for confession. The Bible was written in Greek and Hebrew, and for a more complete understanding, it's often important to discover what the original words really meant. The Greek word for confession is made up of two root words: one meaning "the same" and the other meaning "to say." Thus, confession means to say the same thing as God says about sin. And what does God say? He says: (1) sin is wrong, (2) sin is forgiven. When we confess our sins, the Holy Spirit applies the forgiveness that has already been earned by Christ at the cross and we start experiencing it.

So, the first thing I urge Christians who have problems with sex to do is to confess their sins to God. The second thing I encourage them to do is to put Jesus Christ as the center of their sex lives. What does that mean?

Jesus Christ is more concerned about your sex life than you are. I know some of you will find this hard to believe, but it's true. Putting Christ at the center means trusting Jesus Christ in every area of your life. It means allowing the Holy Spirit, the source of your strength, to give you the power to say "no" and to control your life. It means allowing God to direct you in cultivating the Christian sexual mind as we described in chapter five. And when the Spirit does, you'll find sexual success before marriage (in control) and after marriage (in freedom).

Forgiveness on three levels

Up to this point, I've talked individually to those of you who are non-Christians and then to you who are Christians. Now, I'd like to speak about forgiveness in more detail. Many counselors I know feel the No. 1 hang-up in the areas of self-acceptance, self-concept, and relationships with others is lack of forgiveness—forgiveness on three levels: God, self, and others. We have already talked about forgiveness from God. He promises to forgive us. Jesus Christ paid the price for our sins. Forgiveness is

settled and we can experience it. God
says it, and I believe it, because I've read it,
heard it, and personally experienced it.
That's level one.

The second level is self. Many people have
a hard time forgiving themselves. They
feel like they've botched life so badly that no
one can forgive them. Let's examine this
attitude. If the Creator of the universe says
you're forgiven; if he has wiped the record
clean, then you are forgiven. God forgives
you. Do yourself a favor; forgive yourself. God
still loves you. He still accepts you. He
says you're forgiven.

If it would help, write out the statement,
"I am forgiven by God and I forgive myself.
God has given me a new clean life. He
loves me and I love myself, too." Then say the
statement aloud. What you read, hear, and
say *can* and *does* affect you. Writing, reading,
speaking forgiveness may provide the
impetus you need to accept forgiveness. If
you'd like, check out the Scriptures on
this subject. Read: 1 John 1:9; Psalm 103:12;
Isaiah 43:35; Hebrews 10:16-18; 1 John
2:1, 2.

Level three concerns others. And on this
level, there are two parts. One is the
forgiveness of others—those who may have
hurt or abused you in love, sex, or in
other ways. Not only do we have authority to

do this, we have the responsibility to
do so. The Lord's Prayer says: "Forgive us our
debts, as we also have forgiven our debtors."
Do you know what you are saying when
you say those words? You're asking God to be
as gracious and loving and forgiving
with you as you are gracious, loving, and
forgiving with others. If, after our prayers,
we go out with an unforgiving heart
toward others, it's spiritual hypocrisy.

In the Gospel of Matthew, Christ talks
about forgiveness. When Peter asks how
many times he should forgive someone, Jesus
says not seven times but seventy times
seven. The multiplied answer of 490 is not
important; it's the principle of the thing.
Forgive a person until you have lost count.

An unforgiving heart causes bitterness.
The longer you are unforgiving, the longer
this "root of bitterness" will grow in
you until finally it consumes you. And that
will destroy you as well as your relationship
with those around you.

Now, I'm sure some of you have been
deeply hurt by others who have not even
bothered to come and ask your forgiveness.
God wants you to forgive them anyhow.
Nowhere in Scripture does it say, "Only
forgive them if they come to you; otherwise,
don't forgive them at all." At this point,
your forgiveness benefits you more than

it does them. It clears the decks in your life to get on with the business of living and loving. It frees you from bitterness to partake of God's abundant life.

The other side of the coin

The second part of forgiveness with others is receiving forgiveness. Jesus taught that if you have something against your brother or sister, you are to drop what you are doing and make it right. If we have wronged a person, I believe in most cases it's important to ask forgiveness and then accept it. I say "most cases" because I think there are some instances in which asking forgiveness may open old wounds. Like going to an old girl friend whom you haven't seen for twelve years and who is happily married, and bringing up an unpleasant memory that she may never have shared with her husband. I think you and the Holy Spirit need to make the decisions in those areas.

Forgiveness is important. Forgiveness is biblical. Some of the great personalities in Scripture were people who were in desperate need of forgiveness. David, called by God a man after his own heart, committed adultery with Bathsheba and then had her husband killed in battle so he could marry her. David's confession of his sin to God is recorded in the beautiful Psalm 51

passage. God forgave him and continued to
use and bless him.

The Apostle Peter denied Christ three
times at a crucial moment in history.
Yet God forgave him and made him an
integral part of the early church. The Apostle
Paul was responsible for the death of
hundreds of believers before his conversion.
But God forgave him. And these are
only three of the many instances recorded
in Scripture. God is in the business of
forgiving and we need to accept his love and
grace.

Granted, even though we are forgiven,
there may be some consequences of our sin
remaining. If you were responsible for a
woman becoming pregnant and she gave the
baby up for adoption, you would always
know that somewhere a child of yours existed.
If you lost your virginity so long ago
you can't remember when, some of those
memories will linger. But Christ has an
amazing way of healing even memories so that
the consequences of past sins will not
immobilize you.

R. C. Sproul, a friend of mine who works
with students in the Pittsburgh area,
says that you can get back your lost virginity
or chastity. That's right, you can have it
back again. Obviously, you can't reclaim it
physiologically or historically, but spiritually

and psychologically you can. For God says in his Word that when he forgives you of your sin, he forgets it. God buries it in the deepest sea and to him, you are chaste again. And because of that, you don't have to continue to carry your grief over sexual sins. You are free to move forward as a new person. God has forgiven and forgotten.

That's another great attribute of God. Not only does he forgive, he forgets! He wipes your slate clean. You can feel fresh and new and clean, regardless of how sordid your past. Your newfound good intentions can become a reality because of Christ's love and the unmerited favor he sends your way. Getting a fresh start is usually an attainable dream. Through confession and Christ's sacrifice on the cross, it can be your reality.

Now that you have a fresh start, let's talk about where to go from there. In the next two chapters, let's take a look at dating and mating.

7

DO MEN RESPOND DIFFERENTLY THAN WOMEN?

♥

Do you remember your first date? I sure do. I was so excited I started taking a bath at 4:30 P.M. I mean I got my sister's bubble-bath, flooded the tub, and literally scrubbed myself everywhere! Tying a tie for the date was a big deal. I had to give myself a half hour for that event. I tied the thing seven times just to make sure it hung perfectly. And then the hair! Every hair had to be just right. I got my sister's mirror (the one she used to search out last-minute zits), held it carefully behind my head, and searched for stray hairs that needed to be plastered down with a little more Vitalis.

And then the cologne. Boy, was that important. The first time I put on cologne, I had no idea how much to use. I have a sharp older brother who used to buy expensive colognes, and on the night of my first date, I sneaked into his room (with the attitude "if a little bit is good, a whole lot is better"), and went to work with a variety of his bottles. I smelled like a cologne factory by the time I left the house.

On my first date, I walked from my house to hers to pick her up. I was so nervous I thought I was going to vomit in the nearest bush. A walkway led into her house from the sidewalk. It looked so big and so long, and I was so scared I walked around the block one more time before taking the hike up that huge sidewalk. I remember going to the door and ringing the bell. There I was— almost drowned in cologne, just about to vomit in the bushes, and hoping no one would answer. But someone did—her dad. "Hi, I'm Josh," I said meekly. "Come on in," he answered. I think he may have been as nervous as I was (it was also his daughter's first date), but he didn't show it. "Thank you, sir," I said. And there we sat in deep silence punctuated by short questions and shorter answers.

"How's school going, son?"
"Very well, sir."
"How's the football team doing?"
"Hmm, not so well, sir."
"How's your dad doing?"
"Very well, sir."

And then she came in. I mean, she was next to the most beautiful woman I'd ever seen. She must have started getting ready at 3:30!

We walked to the local theater. It wasn't the most enjoyable evening I'd ever had because I was so nervous, but I was proud as I opened my billfold with my ten one-dollar bills (I got a ten-month advance on my allowance) and held it, a la Rockefeller, as though it contained the total value of the U.S. Mint.

Sitting in the theater was uncomfortable. I didn't know whether you talked to your date in the movie or not. I started to sweat profusely. I whispered into her nose and thought it was her ear. It was a memorable evening.

But as we all know, after the first date you get more experienced and more forward. All week long you'd think about holding her hand. And the next time you went over to her house, you'd call her dad "George" instead of "sir." Then the next time in the theater, you'd plan your big move. You'd scoot back in the chair, brace your left foot, raise your right shoulder and kind of nonchalantly slip your right arm around her shoulder. And you'd sit there in that terribly uncomfortable position trying to watch the show. Ten minutes later the shoulder pains would begin, starting at the top of your shoulder and slowly moving down your arm until you thought you'd die before the film ended.

But, as time moves along in the dating process, the high of "putting your arm around her shoulder" begins to wear off and you have to move to other things. Progress continues. . . .

Once the physical contact starts...

All of us have those memories. I've been forced to tell them from the male perspective, but I'm sure you women have your own stories and your own feelings. Regardless of where you dated or whom you dated or what you did on your dates, there is one similarity —physical progression. And that progression involves what I call the Law of Diminishing Returns. One kind of physical contact satisfies for awhile and then it starts to wear off. And then you have to have a little more and that starts to wear off. Then a little more and a little more. You go a little further and a little further still, and before you know it, you've gone too far.

It's natural to date. And because of the God-given feelings we have for touching and caring, it's also natural to want to reach out and touch that other person. But there are dangers in dating and touching. And as individuals desiring God's best for our lives, we need to be aware of this desire for

physical progression and the Law of
Diminishing Returns.

Whenever I talk about progression and
diminishing returns, people always ask,
"OK. Then tell us—how far is too far? How
far can we go? How much can we get?
Can I touch the knuckles, the wrist, the
elbow? Can I go as far as the shoulders,
as far as the . . .? How far can I go?"

Many people want me to give them a
standard. But giving everyone a standard
would be one of the worst things I could
do. Because some people would go right out,
get a date, skip all the preliminaries,
immediately go to the furthest reaches of the
standard I'd set, and then figure out ways
they could break it. That's how many of us
are.

By now, I'm sure you know I believe
everyone ought to have a standard. And I
think most of you can guess what my standard
is. If not, check out the New Testament.
But what the issue finally boils down to is a
question of the will. What do you really
want out of love and life and sex and marriage?
That will determine how far you go and
what you do. And once you set your standard,
you need to be keenly aware of two things.
One, remember that once you do something
two or three times, it's pretty hard to stop.
Once you get that ol' motor running,
it's pretty hard to turn it off. Remember the

Law of Diminishing Returns. What turned you on a month ago will seem pretty tame tonight.

Setting your own standards

The dating game, the progression principle, and the Law of Diminishing Returns have to involve your most important sexual organ—your mind—if you're going to succeed in male-female relationships. And by "succeed," I definitely don't mean to "score." I mean to feel good about the dating experience: to have an absence of guilt and a good positive feeling about your date, yourself, God, and your future.

It means sitting down beforehand in a nonsexual environment and deciding what marriage means to you. It means looking at the true purpose of sexual foreplay, which is to prepare each other for the ultimate encounter—physical intercourse. It means planning the evening in advance so you don't wind up in a compromising situation, in a place you'd rather not be. It also means understanding yourself and the opposite sex. As your understanding grows, so will your standards.

In chapter five, we talked about some of the sexual differences between a man and a woman. Let's recap some of those conclusions. One big difference was in what turns them on. As Dr. Gearhart Dirks said to me,

"Women are basically programmed by touch, and men by their eyesight." As my friend Ken Poure, a popular youth speaker from Southern California, says, "Breasts are the sex symbols of femininity in our world. So, a girl who is well endowed, wearing a T-shirt that says, 'Pinch me, I'm real,' makes it very difficult for a guy to maintain his cool." However, women don't have to be well endowed or wear message T-shirts to turn a guy on.

I think most women know what's provocative and what's not. They know that how they look helps to turn a guy on. And because of this, I suggest women think seriously about what they wear on a date. What they choose sends off all kinds of signals.

And, if a guy is trying to keep the relationship from becoming overly physical, he needs to be alert to what he's doing with his hands. I'm not advocating a total hands-off policy. But, guys, remember, touch is what turns a girl on, and if you want to be a responsible date, you need to exercise caution in this area.

Another difference is in the area of sex and love. In my experiences talking to men and women, I'm convinced that "sex" is more dominant in the mind of a man, and "love" is more paramount in the mind of the woman.

Let me give you an example in marriage.

Let's say the husband is at work and sees a woman in a tight sweater. Boom . . . all he can think about is sex, S-E-X. He goes to the drinking fountain sex, he goes to the coffee break sex, lunch break sex, all he can think about is getting home.

He drives home through a sex light and charges into the house where he discovers his wife has had a bad day. She drove the car through the garage, burned a hole in his shirt, dropped a dozen eggs, and has a headache that not even a television commercial can cure. The last thing on her mind is sex. And unless the husband is patient and tender and takes the time to slowly bring his wife to his intensity, tension will develop. And, by the way, that's why learning self-control before marriage pays off after marriage.

Now, let's put the wife in a similar situation. She's at work and sees a man in a tight sweater and it may do nothing for her. But perhaps during the day she remembers a loving touch from her husband and as she dwells on that, she begins to think about love. L-O-V-E. She goes to coffee break love, typewriter love. She can't even wait until the day is over. At the lunch break, she jumps in her car and drives home, only to discover that her husband has had a bad day. He has dropped the pancake batter all over his newly waxed floor, burned a hole in her skirt while ironing, and, out of frustration, has ripped the handle off the refrigerator. The television doesn't work and he can't watch his favorite soap opera—"General Hospital." The last thing on his mind is sex. But, with loving words and tender caresses the wife says, "Honey, how are you?" . . .hubby is ready!

Believe it or not, my preposterous illustration communicates two truths: the seeing-male, touching-female emphasis and the whole area of timing. Guys seem to have the ability to get charged up quickly. A woman's sexual interest and energy builds more slowly.

This is important from two standpoints. Women should understand the nature of men . . .realizing that the man may experience high sexual feelings even before the woman does. What may seem purely innocent to the girl may be charging up the guy. And I think men need to realize that a woman can be turned on through touch and kind words and that what might seem innocent to you—some sweet words of love that you read in a Sidney Sheldon novel, and a soft touch—may be arousing her more than you intended.

In summary, let me say that the sex drive is good, created by God to enable a man and a woman to experience an unparalleled relationship based on mutual trust, love, and commitment. But when sex is handled irresponsibly, problems arise. It is my prayer that with an understanding of the process of progression, the Law of Diminishing Returns, and the sexual differences between a man and a woman, you can control rather than be controlled by this God-given gift. Now, let's move to specifics in dating.

8
WHAT MAKES DATING FUN?

♥

Think back for a moment to the times in your life and dating experiences you remember as being the best, the happiest, the most satisfying, and the most carefree. I'll bet most of them are times when you were involved with other people, even older adults, in laughing, listening, and just plain kidding around. These fun times weren't exactly your typical date but, really, that's the point. For dating to feel fun and free, sensual ploys and "games" can't be the main focus. A memorable and happy date is one on which both people are able to freely be themselves.

The constant feedback I get from men and women in my mailbox and in personal conversation reveals that most dating misses

this objective by a mile. Sensual ploys
and sexual gamesmanship—exploitative
love—is the rule, rather than the exception.
No wonder so many people experience so
much heartache in dating. Dating is supposed
to be fun, and it can be if you understand
the purposes of dating and set some goals for
yourself.

Dating for the right reasons

One of the first things a man or woman
must do is to think through his or her
purpose for dating. Sure, responding to the
basic attraction of a person of the opposite
sex is a fundamental reason people date.
But there are a lot of guys and girls who really
aren't ready to date, because they haven't
thought seriously about what dating is for and
what they want it to be in their lives.

You may say, "Come on, everybody dates.
It's only the normal, natural thing to do."
That's true, but beyond the mere response
to intense peer group pressure, why date?

One of the first purposes is socialization. As
we mature, our skills in interpersonal
relationships, conversation, and understanding need to grow up with us. Dating is
a terrific way to learn more about yourself, to
become skilled at sensing the needs and
feelings of another person, and to learn how to
turn that insight into responsive action.
Good dating prepares you for a happy,

growing, and lasting marriage. Poor dating habits breed the fragile and short-lived marriages with which we're all too familiar.

Of course, the second key purpose for dating is mate selection. And one thing is rather obvious: the person you marry will be one of the persons you dated. The typical progression is from casual dates to friendship dates to steady dating to engagement to marriage. It rarely happens any other way. So, dating serves to cultivate and sharpen your tastes, and improve your ability to recognize the character and personality qualities which best mesh with your own. It's a chance to see if the kind of person you *think* you'd like to spend the rest of your life with really *is* the kind of person you'd like to spend the rest of your life with.

At this point in your understanding of the secret of loving, it should be quite obvious that the focus of dating is not sexual exploration, technique development, or conquest. Nothing short-circuits a growing friendship and quality interpersonal communication like premature physical involvement. In *Eros Defiled,* author John White points out, "Premarital sexual excitement too often becomes all-important, as many unmarried couples have discovered. It blocks the very communication it is designed to promote."

"Why?" you ask. Because that's the way

God, the "Manufacturer," created man. When God fashioned man in his own image, he built within him a primary need for divine interaction and fellowship. To make this possible, he created at the very center of man a spiritual capacity; an ability and drive in the spiritual realm, every bit as potent and natural as man's sexual drive in the physical realm. This spiritual ability is unique to man. No other creature of creation has this same urge and capacity.

The reason we sometimes fail to recognize the importance of this spiritual capacity is that, in our arrogance, we've chosen to ignore God and his principles and to put our own desires and will in God's place. The result is always profound separation and alienation. The "spiritual light" goes out at the very center of our being. And we're left groping for the essence of life. The religious quests and longings which fill the pages of human history testify to the reality of this incredible loss.

It only stands to reason then, that if a man and woman wish to experience a maximum oneness, it will have to include mutual and intimate communion on the spiritual level. That's one of the goals of marriage. And since dating is a process that prepares us for marriage, it becomes a priority goal in dating as well. Without spiritual oneness, there can never be complete sexual oneness and fulfillment. Sexual intercourse, you'll recall, was designed by God to be an outward expression of this inward reality between two people.

The interface of two personalities

The second area of union between a man and woman is on the soulish level. We've mentioned this before. It's the coming together of personalities. It's the interface of attitudes, values, goals, likes, dislikes, idiosyncrasies—all the facets that make you fun, likable, and uniquely you. Many of the "love, *because of*" qualities people see in each other exist on this soulish level. And those undesirable negative qualities hidden away in each one of us reside here also. These are the personal liabilities which are only overcome by "love, *period*."

The dating process, leading up to engagement, is the optimum time during which soulish oneness, alongside spiritual oneness, can begin to develop. As two people move toward the marriage commitment, they have an optimum opportunity to discover whether the love they have for each other is truly "love, *period*," a love which sees, but chooses to accept the negative traits they begin to discover within each other. Premature physical involvement clouds this growth process.

Obviously, the third area of oneness

between a man and woman is physical oneness
—sexual intercourse. When sex is a consummation of the spiritual and soulish union
which has gone before, it is the ultimately
satisfying, explosive, and creative sharing
everyone seeks, but few experience. This
is true sexual freedom. Any other path to it
doesn't work. As John White says, "We
live in a world where everything has a design
and function. You don't set a fish free
from the ocean (poor fish, so confined and
restricted) or birds from the necessity of
flight. Birds were designed to fly and fish to
swim. They are freest when they are doing
what they were designed to do. In the same
way, your body was not designed for
premarital sex and will never be truly free
when you engage in it."

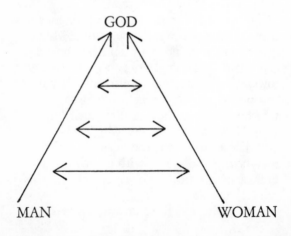

So then, we could picture the dating process like this. As it emphasizes the focus of spiritual growth and development for each person—as they draw closer in communication individually with God—they are automatically drawn closer to each other.

The experience of this truth in your date life will produce some of the most satisfying relationships you've ever enjoyed. In fact, you'll have to be a bit cautious at first that you don't mistake the euphoric "spiritual" feelings you share with another person for true "marital" love at last. They may be. But they could also be simply your first encounter with a man or woman in a relationship as God intended it.

The roles are different

Now, before we explore some of the specific activities that can make dating so much fun, we should look at one more basic pattern God built into men and women when he created them. God designed man to be the spiritual leader in marriage and woman to be the spiritual challenge or responder. The man's assignment is to provide a kind of leadership to which the woman can respond wholeheartedly. The roles are not competitive, they're complementary. He is to provide a leadership saturated with "love, *period*." She is to be set free by this leadership to make a happy, reasoned, and creative response. And contrary to the horror some in the women's liberation movement find in this idea, God's design provides for the optimum development of the personal worth, potential, and uniqueness of both the man and woman.

In the dating relationship, a guy can begin to practice and understand godly initiation and leadership. And a woman can learn how to respond to a man. Obviously, if they have already decided to reserve sexual sharing for their lifelong partner in marriage, thus eliminating it as a focus of tension in the dating process, their dating relationship can be truly free, fascinating, and fun!

Amazingly, even today's "sexually liberated" people who couldn't care less about the spiritual dimension of life are learning that a friendship free of sexual games is very rewarding. In an April 1978 article for *Mademoiselle* magazine, Blair Sabol candidly relates a conversation with a girl friend who expressed surprise that Blair hadn't gone to bed with her man on the second date. Blair commented, "I was astounded. Here we had had what I thought was one of the most intimate evenings merely talking one-on-one and I had felt more satisfied in our sharing each other's personal war stories than in sharing a bed. . . .Before, I would have chalked off this evening as a failure because talking meant merely sparking a good friendship. And friendships supposedly were great to have, only between you and your dog. But between male and female, it usually meant once a friend, never a lover....I am only interested in men I can...have a good conversation with.... Perhaps my new erogenous zone is my mind. Now I want my cerebrum stimulated."

What's the first focus of dating?

Dating is fun when it provides a climate in which two people can become friends. Going to a movie on a first date, then, is generally counter-productive. There you sit for two hours, side by side in a darkened theater, being entertained but never communicating. It's hardly the climate for getting to know one another. Save the movies for later.

A better choice would be to visit a museum or exhibition, walk around a zoo, or window-shop the "period" stores in that old restored section of town. Activities like these provide plenty to talk about and allow you to discover each other's tastes and previous life experiences. And you don't have to sweat being a good conversationalist. The topics of conversation are ready-made.

One of the most fun dates I ever had was to visit a cemetery. We had a hilarious time walking about, reading the comments on the old tombstones. It was a good time I'll never forget. And in case you're short on ideas for creative dates, let me suggest a few. Some on the following list are quite common.

Others will catch your imagination. In either event, remember your own ideas will work the best for you. And the best ideas are those dates which help you communicate and get to know each other more intimately. A good dating activity is one which helps you see and savor new delights and the depth of one another's personalities. These ideas will also stimulate married couples who, hopefully, will never stop "dating" each other.

Play table games, work puzzles.
Engage in simple sports like ping-pong, croquet, or horseshoes.
Go sailing, surfing, swimming or try other water sports.
Take a walk through the neighborhood, a shopping area, or a new section of town.
Do common things together: grocery shopping, laundry, or washing the car.
Find some underprivileged children, orphans, or the kids next door and take them on an outing or picnic. Teach them a new craft or skill.
Make dinner together at her house or yours.
Play recreational sports: golf, tennis, racquetball, bowling, roller or ice skating.
Get involved in a community service project, fund-raising jog-a-thon, or aid project for the elderly or disadvantaged.

Ride bicycles, shoot pool, play miniature
golf.

Visit a local state or national park. Talk
with the rangers, view the exhibits and
points of interest, and hike wherever
you can.

Pick a topic you both know nothing about
and spend a couple of hours at the library
discovering what you can about it.

Identify the skills you'd like to learn from
each other and take turns being the teacher.

Tour some local industries and watch
something being manufactured.

Do some crafts together. Make gifts and
Christmas presents.

Pick a theme and set out to take pictures in
your area of interesting old buildings,
doorknobs, kids playing, unusual cars,
elderly people, stained glass windows, or
signs with odd messages.

Build and fly a kite.

Take a walk in the rain.

Visit a shopping center with a cassette
recorder and interview some children,
adults, or older people.

Spend a Saturday tape-recording unusual
sounds.

Plan a party together and invite a collection
of each other's friends.

Think of a hard-to-find object and hunt for it.

Haul out the family albums and get

acquainted with each other's "roots."
Go to church services and other church
functions together.
Take a train to a nearby town and go
out for lunch or dinner.
Buy a bus pass and ride all over town.
Go to a live musical, symphony, or theater
event.
Attend an auction.

These are only a small fraction of the
activities that can make for great dates. For
more ideas specific to your area, look in
places like these:

Ask your local Visitors Bureau or Chamber of
Commerce for a list of the places tourists
visit in your area.
Check the local museums, universities, and
civic center for a listing of upcoming
lectures, exhibits, or attractions.
Look in the "calendar" section of your
newspaper.
Call the public affairs director of your local
radio or television station and ask what
special events are going on in your area.
Ask your friends for their ideas.

As I indicated earlier, the best ideas are
the ones you invent yourself. Be creative. Let
your imagination go wild. You'll come
up with some great ones.

Overcoming the problems

With these purposes and ideas for dating well in mind, let's talk for a moment about some of the common problems and rough spots. For example, I've met a lot of guys or girls who complain that their date, in an effort to be spiritual and keep things under control, spiritualizes everything. While I can appreciate their concern, imbalance is never the best answer. If God's Spirit is alive in your life and Jesus Christ is important to you, it's only natural that you'll talk about it. But it probably isn't natural that this topic would always consume the entire time you're together.

A lot of couples find that taking a moment to pray together is a beautiful way to begin and/or end a date. And mixing in dating activities which focus on mutually held spiritual values, commitments, or goals is an important facet of dating. After all, biblical values should be the core of life.

Another essential in dating, especially if you are beginning to date someone steadily, is to involve him or her with your family and circle of close friends. If the relationship grows into a marriage, you'll not only be marrying that individual, you'll be joining his family. And if things are uncomfortable there, you'd better learn this and understand why before you contemplate a permanent union. Observing

how a person relates to his or her folks
can reveal a lot about how well this individual
handles intimate relationships and conflict
in those relationships. What you learn
can save a lot of grief later.

And here's another suggestion which is
especially useful if you're not interested in
starting a relationship with a particular
guy or girl, or you aren't being asked out
frequently enough, and yet you still want to
build some friendships with the opposite
sex. If you are a girl, get with a couple of
your girl friends and plan an evening or
afternoon picnic. Invite over four or five guys;
or vice versa, guys go together and invite
over some girls. Keep the numbers uneven to
avoid the tension of having to pair up.
Focus on just having some fun together.

One of the aspects of the culture in which
you and I live is that anything goes. It
can get us into trouble, but it has also
produced a lot of new dating options. Women
can more freely initiate in the dating
relationship. And, in balance, it's a good
thing. Sharing the expense of some dating
activities no longer offends the old macho
image we men were expected to keep up.
And all of us are less role-conscious and more
concerned about being aware and supportive
human beings. In the dating relationship,
that's a great bonus.

A startling realization

Before I was a Christian, I wasn't gross (even though some women called me "octopus"). After I became a Christian, I started to date a Christian woman, and after the sixth or seventh date, I figured I deserved something in return; so, I started to make a little move with her. And she said "nope." I thought she was kidding, so I tried again. And she said "nope" again!

Boy, that ticked me off, because not too many people had ever said "no" to me. So I said, "Who do you think you are?" And she said, "Who in the world do you think you are?" And right there, this liberated Christian woman began to teach me a lesson.

As I began to mature in my relationship with Christ, I began to realize that, first of all, my date was my sister in Christ. And a lot of things I used to do on a date, I wouldn't do with my "sister." In fact, it wasn't long before this perspective broadened into an attitude of always thinking about how I could build up the woman I was dating. How could I leave her a better individual because of the time we had spent together? And let me tell you, men and women, when you date with an attitude like that, dating gets exciting. It's more fun than you've ever imagined.

A good date has a premeditated beginning,

middle, and end. And the entire time is pure joy when you treat the other person in the same way you would want someone to treat the individual you will someday marry. You won't find a better way to love your date or the man or woman he or she will eventually marry. And you'll be doing yourself an enormous favor in the process. You'll be learning how to better love with God's divine "I love you, *period*" love. You'll be growing into more the "right" kind of person—one to whom God can entrust his prized son or daughter as your marriage partner for life.

Is that promise worth the commitment? Is this reward worth the work and the wait? Let's weigh the cost.

9
WILL YOU GO FOR IT?

♥

A well-known actor, famous for his romantic roles, was being interviewed on a television talk show. The host asked what skills he considered essential for being a "great lover." The star's reply was as surprising as it was profound. "A great lover is someone who can satisfy one woman for all her life, and who can be satisfied by one woman all his life long. A great lover isn't someone who goes from woman to woman. Any dog can do that."

By now it should be quite clear that I believe the secret of loving is first of all possessing and sharing God's "I love you, *period*" love. Second, it is becoming a mature person through the dating and growth experiences of life, so that at the right moment, in the right relationship, God can bring you to the right person—one who can uniquely complement you. And, finally, the secret of loving is sharing intimately with your partner, in the security of the marriage relationship, the ultimate expression of your many-faceted love—sexual intercourse.

Quite simply, that's the goal. That's the game plan. That's what we should go for. So why is something so simple, profound, and appealing so difficult? Why is the path to the goal so littered with the carnage of individual lives and relationships that didn't make it? Why have so many fine people become sidetracked?

Four reasons why people fail

There are several important reasons and I want you to look at four of them. Think of them as the four "D's."

The first is *dumb*. Some people are mindless, stupid, and dumb about love and sex. They blindly wander into a situation unaware of the consequences. And before they wake up to what is happening, they are ambushed.

Recently, I saw a scientific paper on the subject of earthquakes. It had an intriguing title: "If You Build Your House on a Crack in the Earth, It's Your Own Fault." Despite the double meaning, there's an important principle there. Laurence J. Peter, author of the famous *Peter Principle,* puts it this way: "If you do stupid things, you will reap abysmal results."

We teach children that to play with fire is to get burned...that to run in front of a speeding car is to be killed. The same warning needs to be given in the realm of love and sex. If we use poor judgment, if we base our life on principles that aren't true, if we violate the function and purposes God intended for sex, then we reap the results. Generally, it's a lot of hurt, pain, and a diluted, if not a ruined relationship. Dumbness is no excuse. God has given each of us a mind and the ability to use it. To wander carelessly and mindlessly into the potent arena of sex —letting your glands be your guide—is dangerous. It's *dumb.* Ignorantly wading into the swamp is a great way to find yourself up to your neck in alligators.

Reason two is *deliberate.* There are a lot of people who pride themselves on having smarts. "Dumb, I am not" is their motto. This person knows what God says the score is, but deliberately decides to follow his own desires. He's too smart to get caught in the consequences. Or so he thinks. Sure, he knows what the Bible promises—both positive and negative—but Mr. Deliberate has decided that he's a special case. Whatever is supposed to happen only happens to the other guy. "It won't happen to me, I'm special. I won't get hurt. I won't get VD. I won't mess up my future. I won't get a girl pregnant. I'm cool. I'm smarter than the average bear. I can play with fire and not get burned."

There's only one problem with this point of view—it never works. No amount of wishful thinking can alter the principles and priorities God programmed into you and me. The consequences of these principles are as certain as the sexual drives one seeks to satisfy in violating them. Oh, you may seem to be getting away with it—for a while. But deliberately avoiding God's way ultimately leads to disaster. Always!

There's a third reason: *distractions* and *lack of discernment.* As we saw in chapter two, we're constantly bombarded with information overload in the area of sex. Some stimuli are stronger than others. But regardless of how blatant or subtle the message, the point is always the same: "You are a person who has the right to sexual fulfillment. Do what feels good. It's wrong for anyone, even God, to tell you not to."

Writer Tom Wolfe calls this atmosphere the "Me Decade." Everything is focused on *me.* What *I* need and what *I* want. Others have called it the "Age of Narcissism"—a term taken from the Greek legend in which a young man became so enthralled with an image of himself in a pool of water that he did not take the time to eat or drink and wasted away into death. And that's what I think many of us are doing today. We're so enthralled with ourselves that we're dying, instead of living.

This "age of narcissism" pumps out the "Me" messages. Whether it's self-help books like *Pulling Your Own Strings,* or the less direct messages emitted by television shows and commercials; we are bombarded with sexual images and the theme, "If it feels good, do it. You're responsible to no one but yourself."

And because we cannot escape totally from our culture, it's important that we develop discernment. One way is to balance the negative messages you receive with positive ones from God's Word.

I have a friend who writes movie reviews for magazines. Over the past six months, he has become aware of the subtle influences on his mind and values through the secular messages proclaimed in films. He doesn't spend his time reviewing X-rated films, but he's aware that the world's viewpoint on sex is very permissive. And my friend has learned that if he's going to continue to see and review some seventy films a year, he's going to have to spend a proportionate amount of time in extra Bible study and Christian fellowship. Balance is essential. We need to fill our minds with the good in order to survive sexually in the "Me Decade."

The fourth big reason people get sidetracked is *desire* and *lack of discipline*. Probably the most encompassing reason for wandering off God's path is because the benefits of waiting seem so distant and the pleasures of indulging are so immediate. Let's face it, sex can be enjoyable outside of marriage. The passionate foreplay, the explosive climax, the feelings of conquering and/or manipulating your lover. I've met couples who sincerely feel they love each other with a "love, *period*" love, and who are committed to each other outside of marriage. But I'm convinced from the encounters I've had with thousands of these young people, and from what I've read in Scripture, that the long-term results are negative. Whether it is guilt, remorse, or plain sadness that accompanies a break-up with that "committed partner," the long-term results of sex outside of marriage are nothing compared to the benefits that can be enjoyed in the context of marital love.

The problem is, it takes self-discipline to wait. And many of us are unpracticed in the art of discipline. We may have disciplined ourselves for months when we took piano lessons or practiced football, but as we have aged, we've been snared up by the accent on instant gratification.

What is the secret to discipline? There

are no *easy* answers, but I'll give you a couple
of *simple* ones. One is to concentrate on
the goals you desire for your marriage.
Visualize them. Talk about them. Write
them down and review them often. You'll
find your actions conforming to your talk,
writing, and imagination. The opposite is
also true. If you write, talk, and visualize
"making it" with everyone you date,
you'll find your body heading without com-
plaint in those directions. Social scientists
call this teleology—the principle of goals
leading to actions.

A second suggestion is to keep your mind
on Christ and on his words as much as
possible. The closer you walk to Christ, the
more you become self-disciplined. The
more intimate your relationship with him,
the more you seek to please him and the less
time and energy you spend on your own
urges. James comments on this in the Bible.
"Submit therefore to God. Resist the
devil and he will flee from you. Draw near to
God and He will draw near to you." I've
discovered the closer you walk to God, the
more self-discipline and direction he gives
you. It's almost like cause and effect.

Sex in the total marriage

Sexual desire and intensity will modify
somewhat as you grow older. But the need for
self-discipline in the many areas of life

will continue. Earlier, I alluded to the fact that sex was only one-twelfth of the marriage relationship. Let me give you a little more insight on this. In July of 1978, *Ebony* magazine interviewed a variety of couples on the topic of "Sex in Marriage." Here's what some of them said:

Dr. and Mrs. Richard Tyson, co-directors of the Institute for Marriage Enrichment and Sexual Studies in Columbia, Maryland, said, "Sex cannot be separated from the other elements in the total relationship. Sex is important throughout a marriage, though it seems that quantity is more important in the early years. But as time goes by and the relationship begins to mature, quality sex seems more important to couples. A couple may have sex ten times a week, and it may be lousy for the woman and great for the man. She would probably rather have one good sexual relationship a week."

Roebuck "Pop" Staples has been married to his wife, Oceola, for forty-three years. "Sex plays a big and a good part in a happy marriage," he said, "but no marriage can make it off sex and sex alone. You've got to have more than that. The first thing you've got to have is understanding; another is respect. You've got to care for and love each other. But I don't know how you can make it if you are not sexually compatible. A man and a woman have got to send out some vibes to each other; you've got to have good sex in a marriage. A lot of young people think sex is all there is to marriage, but after they see what's happening, they realize that a lot of other things are equally important."

Another excellent observation came from Shirley Robinson, a receptionist at the Lutheran Church, Missouri Synod, in St. Louis. She said, "Marriage must be based on friendship and love, and if God is first in your life, all other things will fall into place. Because we are so compatible in so many ways, we have a very good sex life. There is no problem of communication as there is in many unions. We are able to talk freely about sex or anything else, and this is important to us. A good marriage is not based on physical love and beauty alone. What if a mate becomes physically incapacitated or disfigured? A good marriage can weather such storms and still find sunshine."

These thoughts make my point: the quantity of sex may diminish over the years, but the need for quality will continue. And to have quality sex you must have love, patience, and self-discipline—the desire to give rather than to get. Desires may abate; the need for self-discipline never does. And the patterns of self-discipline which will give you sensitive, dynamic, and fulfilling sex are the patterns you are building right now in your dating relationships.

In looking at these reasons why we fail to achieve what God intended for us in love and sex, we see many negatives: *dumbness;* a *deliberate* flaunting of God's design; *distractions* and *lack of discernment;* overwhelming *desires* and lack of *self-discipline.* But let me assure you, these negatives can turn into positives.

When the noted theologian, Karl Barth, was speaking in America, a group of theologians asked him what was the most significant theological discovery of his life. Expecting to hear a complicated answer, they were surprised when he said, "The most important truth I've learned is, Jesus loves me this I know, for the Bible tells me so."

If there's one statement of affirmation I would want you to retain, it's this: God loves you. Jesus came to earth to prove it and to clear sin out of the way so that we could experience God's highest desire for us—an abundant and ultimately fulfilling life. He wants us to personally know his love daily—to enjoy and share it with others. And he wants us to mature in the way he originally intended us to grow up. He has communicated to us his principles of conduct to protect and provide for our welfare.

He has even gone so far as to take care of our failures when we confess them and accept his forgiveness. Through a personal relationship with Jesus Christ, we become transformed. Our minds are renewed. We are changed. We no longer have to be dumb or deliberate or distracted or destitute of discipline. We are set free to love and serve and live an unparalleled life, whether it's in the bedroom or any other room of life.

That's the secret of loving. There is no other.

Don't miss out. I challenge you
.. GO FOR IT!